GO HANUMAN!

by
Swamini Supriyananda

C·H·I·N·M·A·Y·A B·A·L·A K·A·T·H·A

Hanuman leads the monkey army
We're going to find Sita

All our strength
From Sri Ram
All we do
For Sri Ram

Oh no! It's a jungle
We won't quit
If we rest we will rust

Keep going!
Keep going!

**Swing! Swing!
Swing! Swing!**

    **Branch to branch,
        branch to branch.**

        **Sri Ram!
        Jai Ram!
        Jai jai Ram**

Swing! Swing!
Swing! Swing!

Tree to tree,
tree to tree.

Sri Ram!
Jai Ram!
Jai jai Ram

Hanuman leads the monkey army
We're going to find Sita

All our strength
From Sri Ram
All we do
For Sri Ram

Oh no! It's a mountain
We won't quit
If we rest we will rust

Keep going!
Keep going!

Sri Ram!
Jai Ram!
Jai jai Ram

Up!
Up!
Up!
Up!

Climb! Climb!
Climb! Climb!

**Slide! Slide!
Slide! Slide!**

**Down!
Down!
Down!
Down!**

**Sri Ram!
Jai Ram!
Jai jai Ram**

Hanuman leads the monkey army
We're going to find Sita

All our strength
From Sri Ram
All we do
For Sri Ram

Oh no! It's raining
We won't quit
If we rest we will rust

Keep going!
Keep going!

Tip!

Tap! Tip!

Tap!

Tip!

Tap! Wet! Wet! Wet! Wet!

Sri Ram!
Jai Ram!
Jai jai Ram

Squelch! Squerch! Squelch!

Squerch!
Squelch!
Squerch!

Sri Ram!
Jai Ram!
Jai jai Ram

Hanuman leads the monkey army
We're going to find Sita

All our strength
From Sri Ram
All we do
For Sri Ram

Oh no! It's an ocean

GO HANUMAN!
GO!

Jump!

Jump!

Jump!

Sri Ram!
Jai Ram!
Jai jai Ram

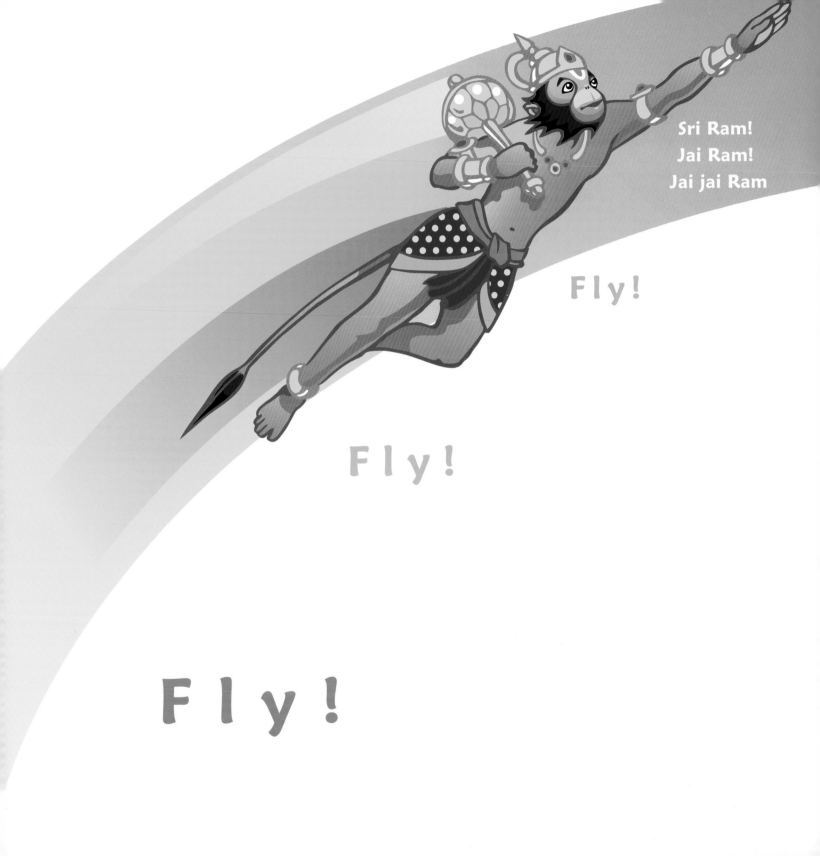

Hanuman finds Sita
Hanuman gives her Ram's ring

Hanuman is a great messenger

All for Ram
All for Ayodhya's King

Quickly back to Ram
We have found Sita

Fly over the ocean –
Fly! Fly! Fly!
Slide in the rain –
Slip! Slip! Slip!

Slide down the mountain –
Slide! Slide! Slide!

Swing through the jungle –
Swing! Swing! Swing!

Find Ram!
Give Him the message!
Give Him Sita's jewels!

Get the army ready
and off we go
Once again...

Through the jungle –
Swing! Swing! Swing! Swing!
Over the mountain –
Climb! Climb! Climb! Climb!
Down the mountain –
Slide! Slide! Slide! Slide!
At the ocean – uh oh!

Oh no!
How do we cross the ocean?
We won't quit
If we rest we will rust

**Keep going!
Keep going!**

We have to build a bridge!

Splash!
Splosh! Splash!
Splosh! Write! Write! Write!

Sri Ram!
Jai Ram!
Jai jai Ram

Jump!
Skip! Jump!
Skip! March! March! March!

Sri Ram!
Jai Ram!
Jai jai Ram

Hanuman leads the monkey army
We're going to find Sita

All our strength
From Sri Ram
All we do
For Sri Ram

Who is THAT?
Ten big heads, a long angry laugh, a very selfish heart!

Oh no! It's Ravana!

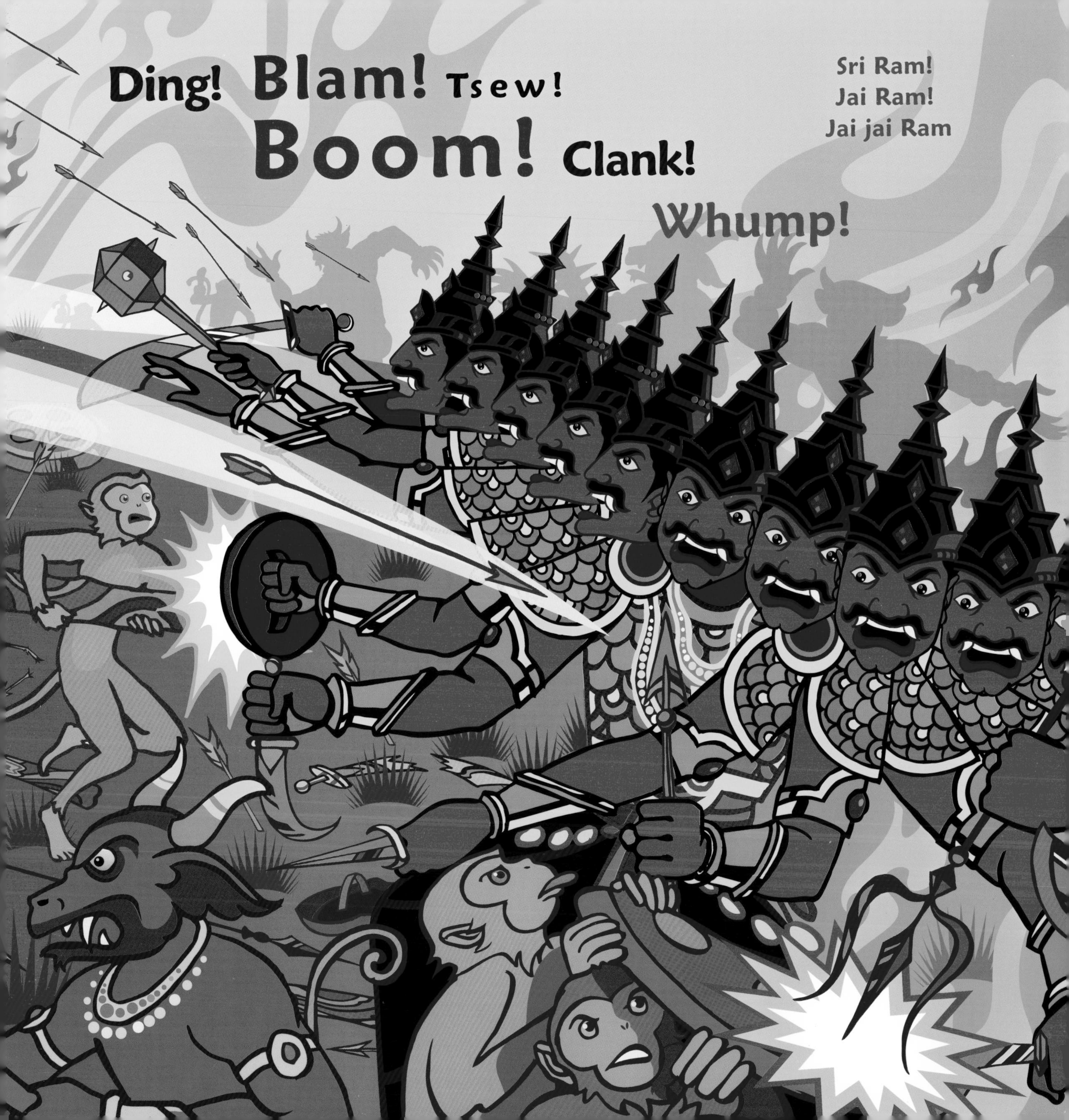
Ding! Blam! Tsew!
Boom! Clank!
Whump!
Sri Ram!
Jai Ram!
Jai jai Ram

Ram defeats Ravana
Now Sita is free
Victory for mighty Hanuman
Victory for you and me!

Hanuman leads the monkey army
He teaches us how to live

All our strength
From Sri Ram
All we do
For Sri Ram

Keep going!
Keep going!

Also in this series-
Hanuman's Big Gig
by Swamini Supriyananda

For ages 5 years and above

CHINMAYA MISSION is a global spiritual organization founded by Swami Chinmayananda with more than 250 centres in 25 countries. For more than 5 decades Chinmaya Mission has served and continues to serve the humanity encouraging holistic growth and happiness through Vedanta.

SHISHU VIHAR

Indian tradition understands the significance of sowing seeds early; in terms of character formation, even as early as the pre-natal stage. Thus the Chinmaya Mission has unveiled a new wing consisting of cultural and spiritual classes for children under the age of 4. Shishu Vihar introduces infants and toddlers to basic concepts that enable spiritual development through cultural education. Classes follow the structure of a modern playgroup where the little participants, under the watchful eye of their respective mothers or guardians, imbibe specific values through songs, stories, and arts and crafts, in a manner appropriate to their age and aptitude. Various props involving an array of colours, shapes and forms are used to relay the information to the kids. Parent and child bond, learn and grow together.

The accompanying mothers or guardians then take the rhymes and stories home and assist with impressing their inner instruction more firmly on their charges' tender, malleable minds. This process generally also sees the same values evoked or reinforced in the entire household.

When the children turn 5, they graduate to the Mission's Bal Vihar programme, which continues to nurture the seeds of spirituality already implanted in them.

Shishu Vihar classes have been running successfully in America, Australia and Southeast Asia since 2011. Look for one close to you, or aim to start one in your area!

More information can be gleaned from the Chinmaya Mission's website for children, **www.chinmayakids.org**, or its institutional website, **www.chinmayamission.com**